MAKE ME WHOLE

An Empty Generation's Need for the Holy Spirit

Bill Pocernich, M.Ed.

Halo ●●●●
Publishing International

ISBN: 978-1-61244-440-6
Library of Congress Control Number: 2015920543

Printed in the United States of America

Published by Halo Publishing International
AP# 726
P.O Box 60326
Houston, Texas 77205
Toll Free 1-877-705-9647
Website: www.halopublishing.com
E-mail: contact@halopublishing.com

CONTENTS

Introduction

What is this book about? If you picked up this book to read it, you likely did it for one of a few reasons:

1. You feel empty. Unfulfilled. Incomplete. Wanting more.

2. You are interested in the Holy Spirit.

3. You are related to me.

I am a married, 43-year-old father of three. I am a high school teacher. I was raised by a loving family. We went to church every Sunday. That continued into my adult life, with a slight break from organized religion in college. I have been a member of churches of various denominations—Catholic, Methodist, Lutheran, and currently, Evangelical Free. Despite growing up in a church and living most of my adult life in a church, it wasn't until recently that the topic of the Holy Spirit was preached. This struck me as a bit odd. Growing up in the Catholic Church, I was taught about the Trinity but never gave it a lot of thought.

I think I'm like a lot of Christians. I am comfortable with God, the Creator. I am equally comfortable with Jesus Christ, His son. But who (or what) exactly is the Holy Spirit? I've known about Him for decades without ever really knowing who He is. He's like the crazy uncle at family gatherings that everyone knows about but most people choose to ignore because he's "different."

Currently I belong to a church that teaches about the Holy Spirit. I was introduced to this "crazy uncle" and even began to develop a relationship with Him. I discovered that although He's different, He's pretty cool. This made me question my previous lack of knowledge on the subject even more. The Holy Spirit is part of the Trinity. He is just as much God as Jesus is. Why didn't I know more about Him before?

I am not special. I think I am a lot like you. I have good days. I also have days that I struggle to live a Christian existence. I want more than that inconsistency from this life, and I think God wants that for me, too. The question is, how can I get that? How can I make my life whole? When examining that question in Scripture, everything kept pointing back to one thing: the Holy Spirit.

The purpose of this book is to examine the most important gift God has given us. It is a gift that is available to us today—the Holy Spirit. A relationship with the Holy Spirit is a life changer, yet so many churches don't feel comfortable teaching about it. It is one-third of the Trinity. Churches I have been to have no problem teaching about God. Jesus? Check. Every Christmas and Easter they really hit that one hard. The Holy Spirit? Crickets. I went through decades of organized religion, and if you had asked me even five years ago who the Holy Spirit was, I couldn't have given you anything beyond a superficial answer. Worse, I think most modern Christians honestly would say the same. I want to remedy that. This book's purpose is to examine who the Holy Spirit is, why we need Him in our lives, and how we can make Him a part of our lives from a scriptural perspective.

This book is written for a broken person, by a broken person, to a broken world. If you are perfect, full, and happy 100% of the time, this book is not for you. If, like me, there are times when you feel like you aren't fully experiencing the joy life has to offer every second of every day, I encourage you to read on.

I am not a professional writer. This is my first attempt at anything resembling a book. Nor am I a biblical expert or even a pastor. My profession is a high school English teacher and basketball coach. That's what I do. That's not who I am. I am a Christian. I am a husband. I am a father to three children. Like you, there are days when I am successful at these roles. Also like you, there are days in which I fail miserably at one or all of them. I am a Christian, not because I'm perfect, but because I'm not. I need Jesus to save me and I need His Holy Spirit to guide me. Without either, I'm lost. Empty. Not whole.

According to the previous paragraph, I have no authority to write this book. I write this book on the authority of Christ. This is the same authority that allows me to fill the emptiness inside of me and allows for you to do the same. Colossians 2:10 states: "And you have been given fullness in Christ, who is the head over every power and authority." This book is about understanding and fulfilling that fullness that is available to everyone. Not just the righteous. Not just the perfect. Everyone. Me. You.

Who am I to write this book? I am a sinner. Through Christ I am forgiven. My prayer is that those reading this book can say the same. If so, you can begin filling the hole inside of you.

Chapter 1

The Hole Inside of Me

Digging the hole

It was a stereo with a dual cassette deck and detachable speakers. We called them "boom boxes" back in the day. It was the first thing I can remember *really* wanting. I had my eye on it for months. I saved up my weekly allowance and birthday money and was finally there. I had enough money to buy it.

I went to the store with my parents, fretting that they would be sold out and the company would refuse to make more (my juvenile mind didn't fully comprehend how capitalism worked). I entered the store. I quickly guided my parents to the electronics section, ignoring everyone and everything else, and went right to the spot. There it was!

"Are you sure this is the one you want?" my mother questioned. How naive. What other one could anyone possibly want?

I humored her insane question by politely responding, "Yes, I'm sure." That's how I remember it, anyway.

I got it home. I took it out of the box. I plugged it in. My joy could hardly be contained. I could record songs off the radio. I could make "mix tapes" of only the best songs from each of my cassettes (I realize that word makes me seem old to some readers, but I digress). It was everything I had hoped for.

That joy lasted a few days. Then one morning I woke up and looked at it a bit differently. It was nice. It was what I had wanted. Yet, I couldn't help but feel disappointed. "That's it?" I wondered. Somehow I thought there'd be more. This stereo was supposed to make my life complete. It had filled my waking thoughts and desires for months. Now I was disappointed. It was a stereo. It was cool. "Now what?" I thought to myself. Instances like this are replayed in society daily:

- The teenager who finally gets a date with "her" or "him."

- The young adult who finally purchases *the* car.

- The mountain climber who reaches the summit.

- The athlete who finally wins the championship.

- The employee who gets the promotion he or she has been eyeing for months.

- The employer who finally reaches the productivity goal for his or her company.

- The child who finally saves enough money to buy *the* toy.

We have all experienced it. We put so much work and thought and effort into a goal. We attain it. There is instant euphoria. Then, after the rush wears off, the dreaded questions: "So, that's it? Now what?"

Depression. Sadness. A feeling that there has to be something more. A feeling that something is missing in our lives. A feeling of emptiness. We try to fill it with another purchase, another goal, another conquest. But the cycle repeats. We never feel totally fulfilled. Why?

The important first step in examining the Holy Spirit is to recognize this feeling. In this chapter I want to scripturally examine why we feel this way and begin to look at how we can finally feel the fulfillment God wants us to feel. You should feel comforted in the fact that we all have experienced this sense of emptiness. You should also be comforted in knowing that God designed us to feel this emptiness, and more than anything, He wants us to choose to feel whole. He can fill that emptiness permanently, and the Bible shows us how.

We all experience this emptiness I described because we were created with a space inside of us for the Holy

Spirit to reside (we will look at scriptural evidence of this in a later chapter). If He doesn't reside there, we feel less than whole and try to fill that void with other things.

Let's look at it another way. I don't know about you, but when I leave church on most Sundays, I feel good. Whole. Complete. However, it doesn't take long for that feeling to end. I propose to you that when I leave church, I am full. I have been in fellowship with the Holy Spirit and He has claimed His rightful home inside of me. Once I leave church, Satan attacks. My fellowship with the Holy Spirit comes to an end, and my mind turns to other, more worldly things. My feelings of emptiness return, oftentimes before I'm even out of the church parking lot. I know I'm not alone in this feeling. Just look at what is going on in the world around us:

- Racial riots.

- Addiction to drugs, alcohol, sex, and pornography.

- People struggling with their sexuality and/or gender.

- Corruption.

- Broken families.

The list goes on. Since Adam ate the forbidden fruit, the world has had problems. It's quite evident that these problems are only becoming more widespread, and they stem from the same place that our feelings of emptiness do. For our purposes here, let's first examine the origin of the emptiness so many of us feel. Genesis 3:1-3 reads:

> Now the serpent was more crafty than any of the wild animals the Lord God had made. He said to the woman, "Did God really say, 'You must not eat from any tree in the garden?'" The woman said to the serpent, "We may eat fruit from the trees in the garden, but God did say, 'You must not eat fruit from the tree that is in the middle of the garden, and you must not touch it, or you will die.'"

At this point, Satan (the serpent) is questioning Eve. Adam and Eve are surrounded by everything they need and want, until Satan points out the one thing they are forbidden to have Genesis 3:4-5 continues:

> "You will not surely die," the serpent said to the woman, "for God knows that when you eat of it your eyes will be opened and you will be like God, knowing good and evil."

Why can't Adam and Eve have that one thing? Satan convinces them it is because God is too pompous, strict, and selfish, that He is a strict, overbearing man. He wants to keep the best things for Himself and not share them. Let's look further at Genesis 3:

When the woman saw that the fruit of
the tree was good for food and pleasing
to the eye, and also desirable for gaining
wisdom, she took some and ate it. She also
gave some to her husband, who was with
her, and he ate it.

Satan convinces Adam and Eve that God was withholding
from them something good, wholesome, and beneficial.
It is interesting to notice that Satan's conversation is with
Eve, while Adam silently stands next to her. Remember
that God spoke His command regarding the tree in
Genesis 2:16-17 to Adam:

And the Lord God commanded the man,
"You are to eat from any tree in the garden,
but you must not eat from the tree of the
knowledge of good and evil, for when you
eat of it you will surely die."

We know that Eve did not hear these instructions from
God because she was not created until Genesis 2:22.

So, what does all of this mean? First, we must
understand that Satan will not attack us where we are
strongest. Here, Satan didn't have his conversation with
Adam, who heard God's instructions firsthand. Instead
he tempted Eve, who likely heard the instructions from
Adam secondhand. Likewise, when we are in fellowship
with the Holy Spirit, we are strong and Satan has no
power over us. He knows that. However, the minute

we take our eyes off of God and make the Holy Spirit a silent bystander, we become vulnerable.

Secondly, we must understand our role as Christians. The world is making it increasingly difficult for Christians to speak the Truth. Here we see, through the example of Adam, what happens when we stand silently by as the Truth is questioned. Adam could have said, "Hold it. God has blessed us abundantly. He cares for us and loves us. He created us in His own image. He doesn't want to withhold goodness from us. It was I He told not to eat from that tree. He has His reasons. We will trust in Him. Get out of here, snake!" But he didn't. He stood by silently as sin entered the world.

Lastly, it is clear that God gives all of us choices. He could have made the fruit of the tree ugly or tasteless. He didn't. He simply gave instructions that, although the fruit is tempting, you are not to eat of it. This may seem unfair until we look at the bigger picture. Adam and Eve were not lacking. Genesis 2:9 makes this clear:

> And the Lord God made all kinds of trees grow out of the ground—trees that were pleasing to the eye and good for food. In the middle of the garden were the tree of life and the tree of knowledge of good and evil.

Satan's trick in Genesis was this: take Adam and Eve's eyes off of all of the good God freely gave to them and focus them on the one temptation they couldn't have.

Then, he made them believe that God withheld, not because it was bad for them, but because He had an ulterior motive.

How often does this happen in our lives? God has blessed me abundantly. I have three healthy children, a loving wife, a nice home, and a stable job. But my focus wanders from these gifts to the things I can't have, either because I can't afford them, they are forbidden, or I haven't been called to that opportunity. Our emptiness comes not from what we lack, but from failing to be cognizant of, and thankful for, what we do have. Read that last sentence again. Biblically, it is stated well in 1 Thessalonians 5:

> Be joyful always; pray continually; give
> thanks in all circumstances, for this is
> God's will for you in Christ Jesus.

God wants us to be joyful always, pray continually, and give thanks for everything. That's simple to understand but unbelievably difficult to do.

I go to church and am thankful for all that I have. That is my focus. I walk out the doors of church and my mind immediately turns to the things I don't have—the nice truck in the church parking lot or the beautiful house across the street. I turn on the radio and listen to a talk show on the way home. As quickly as the Holy Spirit took up His rightful residence for that hour in church, He is just as quickly booted out before I get home. The empty feeling is back, and I search to fill it.

When we are feeling empty is when Satan will tempt us. Being tempted isn't a sin. Satan tempted Jesus in Matthew 4:1-11. Giving in to that temptation is sin. Adam and Eve gave in to their temptation and ate of the tree of good and evil. Why? Not because they were lacking, but because Satan took their minds off of all the blessings God had given them and made them focus on what He hadn't given them. How did it turn out for them? Much like it turns out for us when we give in to temptation. Genesis 3:7-13 records Adam and Eve's reaction:

> Then the eyes of both of them were opened and they realized they were naked; so they sewed fig leaves together and made coverings for themselves. Then the man and his wife heard the sound of the Lord God as He was walking in the garden in the cool of the day, and they hid from the Lord God among the trees of the garden. But the Lord God called to the man, "Where are you?" He answered, "I heard you in the garden, and I was afraid because I was naked; so I hid." And He said, "Who told you that you were naked? Have you eaten from the tree that I commanded you not to eat from?" The man said, "The woman you put here with me—she gave me some fruit from the tree, and I ate it." Then the Lord God said to the woman,

"What is this you have done?" The woman said, "The serpent deceived me, and I ate."

There is a lot of information regarding the emptiness so many people feel in this passage. First, it is important to note that before their encounter with Satan, Genesis 2:25 records that the man and his wife were both naked, and they felt no shame. It was only after they gave in to temptation that they knew shame.

Next, what was their first reaction after giving in to this temptation? Hide! Adam and Eve heard God coming and they ran and hid, though they were not proud of what they did. Satan told the truth when he said Adam and Eve would know good and evil if they ate fruit from that tree. However, Adam and Eve discovered that God was protecting them, not protecting the fruit. He forbade them to eat the fruit for their own good, not for any selfish reason. They were ashamed that they disobeyed God and immediately felt regret.

Their next reaction was also typical. Blame.

"She made me do it."

"It wasn't my fault."

"He tricked me."

They knew. God told them. It was their choice. They chose unwisely because their focus was not on what it should have been.

In this world, we will find what we look for. All of us, if we are honest, can look for things in our lives to be thankful for. Even tribulations create fruits in our lives. Romans 8:28 puts it best:

> And we know that in all things God works
> for the good of those who love Him, who
> have been called according to His purpose.

Adam and Eve ran into trouble when they stopped loving God and instead questioned Him. They ran into trouble because they weren't fulfilling their purpose. Adam was not tending the garden. He stood by silently as Eve was tempted. Eve was not being a good companion. She, due in part to Adam's silence, became an accomplice in the fall of man.

Conversely, we can all find things we can be less than thankful for. Surrounded by the beauty and abundance of the Garden of Eden, Adam and Eve focused on the one fruit they couldn't eat. It is the same for us in our lives. We fail to focus on the blessings and instead focus on what we don't have. This makes us feel empty.

It was true for Adam and Eve, and it is still true today.

Chapter 2

The Hole Inside of Me

Filling the hole

The house my family lives in is a modular home, meaning we had it made in a factory and they brought it out in three sections, then assembled those sections on site. This was in the spring of 2000. My wife was seven months pregnant with our first child in May when they came to set the house. It was a windy day, and to top it all off, we had just received considerable rain the day before, making the ground very soft. The crane used to set the sections on our foundation got stuck several times. It was a stressful day for us!

With the help of the workers, some kind neighbors, and some large equipment borrowed from a construction site nearby, we were able to get the crane where it needed to be to set the house correctly.

When the day was done, the house was set, and the equipment was gone. All that was left was our house and some very long and deep ruts in our soon-to-be yard. I took some dirt from around the house and filled in the ruts. They were still a little rough, but we had a lot of other things to do that summer like finish the house, build our garage, and, oh yes, welcome our first child into the world. The ruts were fine. Not perfect, but fine.

Fast forward to the next summer. I tried to mow our 3.5-acre lawn during the naptime of our now almost one-year-old child. In order to mow quickly, I didn't slow down for the ruts, and our mower and my back took a beating. I discovered that what I had filled the holes with wasn't appropriate. It had settled, and it wasn't the type of soil needed to bring forth a good lawn. It had filled the ruts for a while, but it wasn't lasting. I had to take the time to fill the holes with something else, something better. So it is with us.

It is natural for us, when feeling less than fulfilled, to attempt to fill the emptiness with something. Anything. Doesn't have to be great soil. Just something to fill the hole. The book of Galatians has a pretty complete list in chapter 5:

> The acts of the sinful nature are obvious:
> sexual immorality, impurity and
> debauchery; idolatry and witchcraft;
> hatred, discord, jealousy, fits of rage,
> selfish ambition, dissensions, factions and

envy; drunkenness, orgies, and the like. I
warn you, as I did before, that those who
live like this will not inherit the kingdom
of God.

In the absence of God, in the absence of His Holy Spirit,
we feel unfulfilled. We can have everything the world has
to offer and it won't be enough. We see this often in the
celebrities we adore. They seemingly have it all. They
are the best in the world at what they do, have enough
money to buy just about anything they want, have a
beautiful spouse, yet get hooked on drugs or caught in
affairs and never seem fulfilled or happy. Why?

It's not just the celebrities. Like Adam and Eve,
God has provided for me in abundance. Yet, I still have
moments when I feel unfulfilled, like I need more to
be truly happy. I'm watching a game on TV with my
wife by my side and children there next to me, perfectly
content. Then a commercial comes on for Doritos.
"Hmm. I am a little hungry. I think I'll get some chips."

There. Now I feel better. Life is good again. Then
a truck commercial comes on. "Hmm. You know, that
would be a lot nicer to have than our current car." And
the seeds of discontent grow. The door opens and the
Holy Spirit begins to leave as food and the adrenaline
rush of a new purchase begin to take His place.

Conversely, there are people in this world who
comparatively have very little. Yet these people are
abundantly happy. How can this be?

It is obvious that the rich celebrities (and all of us, at times) have their eye on what they don't have, while the comparatively poor people instead focus on what they do have. Maybe because it is easier. After all, how many things can a modern-day celebrity not have? Pretty short list. How many things does a comparatively poor person have? Again, a short list. Much easier to focus on than the converse, which would be a lengthy list. But there is more to it.

We all have a hole inside of us. It was created by God. Why? 1 Corinthians 6:19 holds the answer:

> Do you not know that your body is a
> temple of the Holy Spirit, who is in you,
> whom you have received from God?

Did you know this? In all of my years as a youth and young adult attending church, I didn't. Your body has a purpose—to house the Holy Spirit! This is where our empty feeling comes from. It's not just a feeling. We really are empty. Our body has a place inside of it built especially for the Holy Spirit. We attempt to fill ourselves with things from the world such as those listed at the beginning of this chapter from Galatians, chapter 5. We try to fill it with food. Still empty. Expensive purchases. Still empty. Extra-marital affairs. Still empty. Drugs. Alcohol. Still empty.

We try to fill it with food. It is okay for a short time, but then we hunger again. We try to fill it with drink. We are quenched for a short time, but then we thirst again.

We try to fill it with material goods. We are happy for a while, until the next "thing we really need" reveals itself.

We can never fill that hole inside of us with worldly things because it wasn't designed to house those things. Sure, they may fill us temporarily, like the bad dirt I shoveled into the ruts, but that fullness we seek won't last. Like the bad dirt, it will settle and fail to bring forth good things. That's not how we were designed. However, that same chapter—Galatians 5—holds the answer to what we can expect when we are filled by the Holy Spirit:

> But the fruit of the Spirit is love, joy, peace, patience, kindness, goodness, faithfulness, gentleness, and self-control.

When I leave church on Sundays, this is how I feel. After my morning devotional time, this is how I feel. When I'm watching the game on TV, surrounded by my family, before the commercials point out the things I don't have, this is how I feel. Content. Loving. Joyful. Peaceful. Patient. Kind. Good. Faithful. Gentle. Self-controlled.

If we are honest with ourselves, we will see that we don't want a perfect spouse or companion; we want love. We don't want to take performance-enhancing drugs to be successful; we want joy. We don't want to have our way; we want peace. We don't want to rush through life; we want patience. We don't want to dislike others; we want kindness and goodness. We don't want to lust after things we can't have; we want faithfulness. We don't want to be angry with others; we want gentleness and self-control. Why, then, do we choose what we don't want over what we do? We will look at that closer in a later chapter.

What we need to realize now is that when we are feeling empty, it is because the Holy Spirit is not working in our lives. When this is happening, it is not because the Holy Spirit willingly left His rightful house inside of us. It is because we asked Him to leave to make room for something else that will live in His house and make us happy. A purchase. Food. Drink. Drugs. A promotion. A forbidden fruit. Whatever it is that takes the Holy Spirit's place in our lives may make us feel good for a short amount of time, but then we will be left feeling unfulfilled. "This is it? Now what?"

Don't get me wrong. There is nothing wrong with striving to be successful in your life. It is perfectly fine to devote time in your life to attaining career and family goals. The point is to make sure that the worldly things you pursue don't take the place of the only thing in your life that can make you feel whole.

The only way you can have a lasting feeling of being complete and whole is by accepting the Holy Spirit into your life and allowing Him to fill the emptiness inside of you. We must reject exalting worldly pleasures and instead turn consistently to the Holy Spirit.

Unfortunately, many people can't do this because they aren't comfortable with who the Holy Spirit is. I know I wasn't, and I was churched in various denominations throughout most of my life. This third member of the Trinity was a stranger to me instead of the best friend He was designed to be. I fear many modern-day churches really miss the mark in terms of introducing Christians to their best friend.

If you're like I was for most of my life—not comfortable with the concept of the Holy Spirit—you're not alone. My fear is that many Christians, in addition to non-Christians, don't know the Holy Spirit more than superficially. Let's figure out exactly who the Holy Spirit is before going any further.

Chapter 3

Who is the Holy Spirit?

Introducing you to your new best friend

I still remember the first time I met my wife. I was a sophomore in college and walked down to the common lounge on the floor of our dorms to pop some popcorn in the microwave. I walked into the kitchen area and saw my wife and a fellow freshman friend of hers at the table studying. I put the popcorn in the microwave and started it. I had three minutes and forty-five seconds to kill, so I thought I'd introduce myself. It was innocent. I wasn't trying to "pick them up." I said hello. They responded with a curt hello, no eye contact, and silence. Crickets. I proceeded to kill the remaining three minutes and thirty-five seconds in the television room of the commons.

Introducing yourself to someone new can be difficult for one reason—we fear rejection. "What if he/she doesn't like me? What if I'm not good enough?"

My relationship with my wife has improved from this inauspicious beginning, but what if I had never tried to talk to her again?

One thing you don't have to fear from getting to know the Holy Spirit is rejection. As we have already discovered, He has a place inside of us especially for Him. He belongs with us. We were created to house Him. But, like any relationship, our friendship with the Holy Spirit must begin somewhere, and it must be nurtured.

As I have stated, it is my belief that most churches fail miserably when it comes to the Holy Spirit. The Holy Spirit is looked upon as a mystical being—part legend, part real, and available only to a select few. This is not true at all. In this chapter, we will examine exactly who the Holy Spirit is and whom He is available to.

First, it is important to understand that the Holy Spirit is a "who," not a "what." The Holy Spirit impregnated Mary with Jesus (Luke 1:35). In John 14:26, Jesus describes the Holy Spirit as a Counselor and a Teacher. These passages clearly describe characteristics of a person, not an object or thing.

Many Christians understand the Holy Spirit as part of the Trinity—God the Father, God the Son, and God the Holy Spirit. They are three separate people in one. God is the creator of the universe. God became a man in Jesus so that Jesus could die for our sins. Jesus rose from the dead to offer salvation for all people who believe in Him in the form of spiritual rebirth. When Jesus ascended into heaven, His physical presence left this earth, but

He promised His disciples that He would send the Holy Spirit to them so they would not be alone (Luke 24:49). This is the Holy Spirit that is available to us today. However, the Holy Spirit was working before Jesus ascended to heaven. The Holy Spirit makes several Old Testament appearances:

- In Exodus 31:1-11, the Spirit gave Bezalel and Oholiab artistic abilities. He also gave the craftsmen of this time the skills needed to make everything that the Lord commanded of Moses.

- In Judges 11:29, the Spirit came upon Jephthah and aided him in military conquests.

- In 1 Samuel 16:13, the Spirit gave David power to rule.

- In 2 Chronicles 24:20, the Spirit came upon Zechariah and gave him the power to prophesy.

We see in the Old Testament that the Holy Spirit was given to specific people to fulfill certain roles to further God's plan. However, Acts 2:17-21 makes it clear that, today, the Holy Spirit is available to all who believe in Jesus Christ as their savior:

"In the last days," God says, "I will pour out my Spirit on all people. Your sons and daughters will prophesy, your young men will see visions, your old men will dream dreams. Even on my servants, both men and women, I will pour out my Spirit in those days, and they will prophesy. I will

show wonders in the heaven above and
signs on the earth below, blood and fire
and billows of smoke. The sun will be
turned to darkness and the moon to blood
before the coming of the great and glorious
day of the Lord. And everyone who calls
on the name of the Lord will be saved."

In the Gospel of John, chapter 14, Jesus also makes it
clear that the Holy Spirit will be with us forever, and
that, although the world as a whole cannot accept Him,
He lives in us and with us:

And I will ask the Father, and He will give
you another Counselor to be with you
forever—the Spirit of truth. The world
cannot accept Him, because it neither sees
Him nor knows Him, for He lives with you
and will be in you.

So, who is the Holy Spirit? He is God. He is Jesus.
He is sent to all believers to counsel us and teach
us. Not only is He available to us, but we were also
created specifically to accommodate Him. Recall that
1 Corinthians 6:19 refers to the body as a temple of the
Holy Spirit:

Do you not know that your body is a
temple of the Holy Spirit, who is in you,
whom you have received from God? You
are not your own; you were bought at a
price. Therefore honor God with your
body.

When we accept Jesus Christ as our savior, the Holy Spirit enters our body and claims His rightful place in our lives. When we are in fellowship with Him, He will guide us, teach us, and make us whole.

Maybe you are thinking, "My life is good. I don't need the Holy Spirit. Sure, there may be times when I feel like I need or want more, but that's healthy. It motivates me to achieve. Everyone feels that way."

I want to challenge that concept right now. It is perfectly fine to feel motivated to succeed. However, when you allow worldly desires to take the rightful place that the Holy Spirit should occupy in your life, you are setting yourself up to live less than the full life God has in store for you.

God desires the Holy Spirit to live inside you. His purpose there is to counsel you and to guide you. We will have scriptural evidence of this in an upcoming chapter. If you allow anyone or anything else in your life to guide or counsel you, you will not feel the fullness that God wants for you. We are all guilty of this. How many times do we allow our worldly desires to guide our decisions? How many times do we do things to please others instead of pleasing God? This will never allow you to feel the consistent fullness God desires you to have.

Many of you think you are fine, that you don't need the Holy Spirit's help. Here's the good news: God doesn't want us to just be "fine." Besides, what does "fine" really mean? I love my wife, and she is a great example of a Proverbs 31 woman, but she is human.

Like all of us, she feels less than full at times. When I sense that she is upset, I will ask, "Honey, what's wrong? It seems like something's bothering you." When she responds, "Nothing, I'm fine," I know something is bugging her. "Fine" isn't what my wife wants her life to be; it isn't what *I* want her life to be. And it isn't what God wants her life to be. Jeremiah 29:11 states:

> "For I know the plans I have for you,"
> declares the Lord, "plans to prosper you
> and not to harm you, plans to give you
> hope and a future."

God doesn't want us to be "fine," whatever that means. He wants us to prosper. He wants us to have hope. If you have recently felt hopelessness, hatred, discord, jealousy, anger, selfish ambition, dissension, or envy in any way, then you need to look closely at what is residing in the place where the Holy Spirit is supposed to be living.

If you looked at that list and thought, "No. I haven't felt any of those things recently. I'm fine," then I challenge you to examine what "fine" is. "Fine" isn't perfect. "Fine" isn't prosperous. "Fine" isn't what we feel when the Holy Spirit claims His rightful place in our bodies and our lives.

As you will see, the role of the Holy Spirit and all He offers to those who accept Jesus into their lives is very clearly stated in Scripture. Here's a clue: making you feel "fine" isn't one of His jobs. He has much more in store for you than that.

Chapter 4

The Role of the Holy Spirit

What purpose He serves

The game was going fine. We were ahead by double digits, cruising comfortably, and then things started to change. Our opponent was making a run, scoring eight straight points to trim a once-comfortable lead down to a more tenuous seven-point lead. Additionally, I was in the unfamiliar role of having an intimate, rooting interest in this basketball game but no control. I was not a player or a coach. I was just Dad. To make matters worse, I couldn't vent to my wife or get angry that the coach had one of her best players on the bench—the coach was my wife. She was coaching our fifth-grade daughter's team, and they couldn't get a rebound. My wife encouraged the girls. "Come on, girls, we have to rebound!" while I thought, "Coach, your best rebounder is sitting next to you. Get her in the game!"

Now, my wife knew this. She was coaching fifth-grade girls basketball and rotating players the best she could, and it was this girl's time to sit down. However, it reinforced for me the importance of roles on teams and roles in our lives.

To this point, Scripture has made it clear that the Holy Spirit is a person whom our bodies were made to house. The purpose of this chapter is to look further at the role the Holy Spirit is supposed to be playing in our lives. News flash: His role isn't to sit on the bench while we wonder why we aren't getting what only He can provide. The Gospel of John spells out many purposes God has for the Holy Spirit. For instance, John 14:26 says:

> But the Counselor, the Holy Spirit, whom
> the Father will send in my name, will
> teach you all things and will remind you of
> everything I have said to you.

He counsels us. He teaches us. He does this by reminding us of Jesus's words and teachings. The world today is a confusing one without the Holy Spirit. It is confusing because there is no right or wrong. Everything is a gray area in which each individual can determine their own decisions. The Holy Spirit reminds us that there aren't *50 Shades of Grey*. There is right and there is wrong.

Children like structure. Sure, they will complain about it when it is in place, but my experience with my own children and those I have taught and coached tells me that children like having clearly set boundaries. They will test those boundaries at times, to be certain, but knowing what is allowable and what is forbidden is a comfort. Knowing someone cares enough to enforce those boundaries is also comforting.

That goes for all of us. We are God's children. With the Holy Spirit in our lives, we will be reminded of the Truth spoken in the Bible and will have a healthy, safe set of rules to follow in our lives—rules not designed to keep us from enjoying all the good that God created, but rather rules designed to help us enjoy all He created in a healthy, safe way, much like the lessons and rules we give our children or that our parents gave us.

John 16:8-11

When He comes, He will convict the
world of guilt in regard to sin and
righteousness and judgment: in regard to
sin, because men do not believe in me;
in regard to righteousness, because I am
going to the Father, where you can see
me no longer; and in regard to judgment,
because the prince of this world now
stands condemned.

The Holy Spirit will convict the world of its sin and call it to repentance. He will do this to save the souls of those who don't believe. My prayer is that those people will listen to the Holy Spirit. We *all* have a place inside of us especially for Him. He is available to everyone, as is salvation.

For the believers, He will set a standard of righteousness. Jesus is no longer walking physically on this earth as an example of righteousness. The Holy Spirit, as Counselor and Teacher, is here to act in Jesus's stead. I fear that many proclaimed Christians don't have the Holy Spirit active in their lives. If we did, we would be judging less and loving more. That is what Jesus called us to do. Matthew 22:36-40 states that clearly:

> "Teacher, which is the greatest commandment in the Law?" Jesus replied, "Love the Lord your God with all your heart and with all your soul and with all your mind. This is the first and greatest commandment. And the second is like it: Love your neighbor as yourself. All the Law and the Prophets hang on these two commandments."

My fear is that Satan's attack on Christians through the media and the modern worldly perspective has hardened the hearts of Christians and turned their focus away from this command that Jesus gave us. Christians need to be in constant commune with the Holy Spirit to remind them of their true purpose and calling. Hearts will be won with love—not judgment, not reasoning, not fear, and certainly not condemnation. Love.

It is important to realize that John 16:11 promises that the Holy Spirit has already judged the prince of this world, Satan. This is a difficult time to be a Christian. We are quickly becoming one of the most persecuted religions, not just in the East, but also in America. We are not to worry. We are not to judge. That has already been done. We are to live our lives with Jesus's love shining through us brightly every day. This is definitely not easy. That is why God sent the Holy Spirit to reside in us. "With man, this is impossible, but with God all things are possible," (Matthew 20:26). We have been given the power to show Jesus's love daily. We need to accept it and use it.

John 15:26

When the Counselor comes, whom I will
send to you from the Father, the Spirit of
truth who goes out from the Father, He
will testify about me."

The Holy Spirit will testify about Jesus. I don't know about you, but this is very comforting to me. If I have the Holy Spirit, I don't need the words to testify for Jesus. He will provide them. He will guide me to live a life that others will look at and wonder, "What's different about him? I want that." His guidance will provide all I need to witness for Christ and testify for Him.

John 16:13

But when He, the Spirit of truth, comes,
He will guide you into all truth. He will not
speak on His own; He will speak only what
He hears, and He will tell you what is yet
to come.

The Holy Spirit will guide us into all truth (how much
we need that today). It seems that there no longer is a
single truth. No matter the instance, there are gray areas
and no real right and wrong. This is true without the
Holy Spirit. The Holy Spirit will guide us into all truth.
He will allow us to distinguish right from wrong, truth
from lies. We need that today as much as we ever have.

John 16:14

He will bring glory to me by taking from
what is mine and making it known to you.

Jesus is speaking in this passage, just as He has been in
the last several. The Holy Spirit will bring glory to Jesus.
How? By taking everything from Jesus and making it
known to us. Wow! We can know everything that Jesus
knew through the Holy Spirit's guidance and counsel.

As all-encompassing as these verses seem to be in
outlining the purpose of the Holy Spirit, there is even
more about His role in our lives in the New Testament.

Romans 8:26

In the same way, the Spirit helps us in
our weakness. We do not know what we
ought to pray for, but the Spirit Himself
intercedes for us with groans that words
cannot express.

The Holy Spirit will intercede for us. When we don't
know how to pray or what to ask God for, the Holy
Spirit will ask God for us. We only need to be in counsel
with the Holy Spirit and ask Him to intercede for us "in
accordance with God's will," as verse 27 continues.

Romans 5:5

And hope does not disappoint us, because
God has poured out His love into our
hearts by the Holy Spirit, whom He has
given us."

Everyone needs to know they are loved. With so many
broken homes and absentee parents, I fear we have a
generation of people that are unsure whether or not they
are loved. Lacking a sufficient earthly example, people
are uncertain if they are loved at all. If the Holy Spirit
lives inside of us, we will know we are loved in an
unconditional way by a loving Father.

Romans 8:2

Because through Christ Jesus the law of
the Spirit of life set me free from the law
of sin and death.

The Holy Spirit gives us the power to live a Christian life. For many people, it is difficult to go through the day without getting angry, envious, jealous, or irritated. For me, it is impossible. The Holy Spirit will give us the power to do this. Without the Holy Spirit in our lives, this is impossible.

Churches today don't teach about the Holy Spirit enough (or in some cases, at all). Because of this, we have a lot of Christians in this world who don't have a relationship with the Holy Spirit. This is causing the world to view Christians in a very un-Christlike way. Ghandi is credited with saying, "I like your Christ, but I don't like your Christians." Why are so many Christians not living a Christlike lifestyle? Without the Holy Spirit in their lives, it is impossible to do so.

1 John 2:26-27

I am writing these things to you about
those who are trying to lead you astray. As
for you, the anointing you received from
Him remains in you, and you do not need
anyone to teach you. But as His anointing
teaches you about all things and as that
anointing is real, not counterfeit—just as it
has taught you, remain in Him.

This may be the most important verse of all. The Holy Spirit helps us discern false teachings. He is the only place to which we can safely turn. Most churches no longer teach that everything in the Bible is the Truth. Our modern culture can't be trusted to morally guide us. Even our earthly parents, who mean well, will lead us astray at times. Only our heavenly Father will lead us safely every time. He will do this through the Holy Spirit. Without His existence in our lives, we are walking alone.

As you can see, the Holy Spirit is supposed to play a vital role in our lives. When we relegate the Holy Spirit to the bench, we will be like the coach imploring her team to rebound when the best rebounder is sitting next to her. Stop wondering why you aren't feeling full. Put the Holy Spirit in the game and give Him the ball. Watch great things happen.

Chapter 5

Hello, Holy Spirit

Inviting the Holy Spirit into your life

My wife had the great idea to take pictures from each of our family vacations and make a collage for each of them. We were going through our old pictures to accomplish this task when we came across a wedding invitation. It was for our wedding.

Now, we've sent out invitations for lots of birthday parties over the years, trying not to forget anyone, but seeing our wedding invitation brought back some anxiety. Birthday parties are easy. I teach at the school. I get an updated class list, and it is pretty hard to miss someone.

Wedding invitations are different. Not only did we have to invite all of our relatives, some of whom we hadn't spent a lot of time with, but we also had to remember old friends, classmates, colleagues, and mentors. We didn't want to forget anyone, but we had to keep the number reasonable as well.

As you look at your life right now, if you were to have a special celebration, who would you invite? The sight of our wedding invitation, now almost eighteen years old, brought that question back to my mind. My thoughts immediately went to my relatives, friends, and colleagues. When you think of your closest friends, is the Holy Spirit on your list?

We have a better understanding of who the Holy Spirit is, we know His role, and we know He is available to everyone. Next question: How can we invite Him to work in our lives? After all, He doesn't exactly have an address we can send a written invite to.

Acts 2

> Peter replied, "Repent and be baptized,
> every one of you, in the name of Jesus
> Christ for the forgiveness of your sins.
> And you will receive the gift of the Holy
> Spirit. The promise is for you and your
> children and for all who are far off—for all
> whom the Lord our God will call."

The verses above make it abundantly clear that, in order to receive the Holy Spirit, you must:

1. Repent of your sins. A simple Google search gave this definition for "repent": *to feel such sorrow for*

46

*sin or fault as to be disposed to change one's life
for the better; be penitent. To remember or regard
with self-reproach or contrition: to* **repent** *one's
injustice to another. To feel sorry for; regret.*

It is clear that admitting your sins isn't enough.
You must be ready to try and leave those sins
forever. You must be so sorrowful for your sins
that you will try to change your life in order not to
repeat them.

2. Be baptized. Baptism could be the subject of
another book. This is not referring to the infant
baptism popular in many churches. There is no
scriptural basis for infant baptism. This is talking
about a baptism you decide to do when you
accept Jesus Christ as your savior. Simply put,
baptism is done when you decide to follow Christ.
Symbolically you enter the water as your old self
and come out of the water anew. Your old self is
washed away.

I am not an expert on this sacrament. However,
the Bible clearly commands us to be baptized. My
personal experience with baptism is that I truly
felt the Holy Spirit's presence when I exited the
water. I felt the fruits of the Spirit enter my life
almost instantaneously: love, joy, peace, patience,
kindness, goodness, faithfulness, gentleness,
and self-control (Galatians 5:22-23). They don't
always remain, because I fail to be in commune

with the Holy Spirit continually. However, I can tell you this: when I make a concerted effort to call upon the Holy Spirit, His fruits enter my life *every time.*

Additionally, this verse makes it clear that this promise was made not just to the disciples and people of that time period, but "for all whom the Lord our God will call." You. Me. Everyone. He will come to us all if we invite Him through repentance and baptism.

The Holy Spirit is available to everyone. He is not here to condemn us. He is here to guide us and counsel us. He is here to help us decipher good from evil and right from wrong. He is here to allow us to have a relationship with God through Jesus Christ. If you want Him to enter your life, you are to repent and be baptized.

Inviting and accepting the Holy Spirit into your life is a life-changing experience. It will not make you perfect. You will still sin. You will still have moments when you feel empty. But you will never again be alone. You will never again be hopeless. As your relationship with the Holy Spirit grows, the grasp sin has on your life will lessen until it is no more. Things will be clearer. Right and wrong will be easier to distinguish.

Just like any relationship, your relationship with the Holy Spirit must be nurtured. Spend time daily in the Bible. There are innumerable devotionals and Bible reading plans available in print or online. Ask for the Holy Spirit's guidance in understanding Scripture as you read. He has been given to us to teach us. Use Him as a resource. Ask His help in prayer. Spend time daily in prayer. If you don't know what to pray for, ask the Holy Spirit to help you.

The Holy Spirit is a person. Treat Him as such. Knowing Him is not a mystery. I have introduced Him to you in this book, if you hadn't been introduced to Him before. Now, do what you would do with anyone else that you want to learn more about. Talk to Him. Find out background on Him. Nurture a relationship with Him by confiding in Him. Always remember that you are not alone. God has provided you a counselor and friend. He has created a place inside of you in which He is to reside.

Who are you to deserve this? You, like me, are a sinner. God loves you. Through Jesus Christ He has forgiven you. He wants you to enjoy all that this world has to offer and has given you a friend to share it with. My prayer is that those reading this don't reject that friend. My prayer is that you accept this gift that God has offered to you and that you begin cultivating a relationship with the Holy Spirit today.

Chapter 6

The Power of the Holy Spirit

What we can expect when the

Holy Spirit enters our lives

As we have discovered, the Holy Spirit was made available to all of us when Jesus left this earth after His resurrection. God created us to house the Holy Spirit, and He made the Holy Spirit available to all who repent and become baptized. Now, let's look at another important question: What can we expect when we nurture a relationship with the Holy Spirit?

Because this third of the Trinity is under-taught, it is often shrouded in mystery. It is my belief that part of the reason people are apprehensive about cultivating a relationship with the Holy Spirit is that they are afraid of what will happen to them if they do.

The Bible tells of people talking in tongues when the Holy Spirit comes upon them. This is weird. I don't want to be weird. I'm fine without this "Holy Spirit." Fine? We already covered that. You are meant to be more than fine!

It is important to know that each of us is created with specific gifts for a certain purpose in God's plan. This is shown throughout Scripture, but it is clear in Romans 12:

> Just as each of us has one body with many members, and these members do not all have the same function, so in Christ we who are many form one body, and each member belongs to all the others. We have different gifts, according to the grace given us. If a man's gift is prophesying, let him use it in proportion to his faith. If it is serving, let him serve; if it is teaching, let him teach; if it is encouraging, let him encourage; if it is contributing to the needs of others, let him give generously; if it is leadership, let him govern diligently; if it is showing mercy, let him do it cheerfully.

As we can see from this passage and others like it, God created each of us differently. I'm not called to talk in tongues. My gift is in teaching. Through counsel from the Holy Spirit you will discover yours. Don't be afraid that asking the Holy Spirit into your life will lead you someplace you don't want to go. Your bigger fear should be that the lack of the Holy Spirit's guidance will keep you from doing the things you should be doing to live a full life.

There are many myths about the world today. Here are a few:

- Only the strong survive.

- You have to be tough to get by in this world.

- You can't be lenient. If you give someone an inch, they'll take a mile. You must be stern.

Let's compare this to what God told Zerubbabel in Zechariah, chapter 4, verse 6:

> So He said to me, "This is the word of the Lord to Zerubbabel: 'Not by might nor by power, but by my Spirit,' says the Lord."

If you want to accomplish something worthwhile and truly lasting in this life, the only way to do it is through the Holy Spirit—not by might, not by power. Only through your friend and counselor, the Holy Spirit.

I am going to quote from a place other than the Bible here. In the movie *Coach Carter*, a character quotes poetry of Marianne Williamson:

Our Deepest Fear

Our deepest fear is not that we are inadequate.
Our deepest fear is that we are powerful beyond measure.
It is our light, not our darkness
That most frightens us.

We ask ourselves
Who am I to be brilliant, gorgeous, talented,
and fabulous?
Actually, who are you *not* to be?
You are a child of God.

Your playing small
Does not serve the world.
There is nothing enlightened about shrinking
So that other people will not feel insecure around you.

We are all meant to shine,
As children do.
We were born to make manifest
The glory of God that is within us.

It is not just in some of us;
It's in everyone.

And as we let our own light shine,
We unconsciously give others permission to do the same.
As we are liberated from our own fear,
Our presence automatically liberates others.

We are called to be great. "Fine" isn't what God wants from our lives or for our lives. Only through the power available to us through the Holy Spirit can God's will for our lives be fulfilled.

You might ask, "What can I expect when the Holy Spirit enters my life?" You can expect God's great and perfect will for your life to begin fulfillment.

Chapter 7

Understanding My Nature

Why the Holy Spirit is needed

Paul puts it best in chapter 7 of his letter to the Romans:

> I do not understand what I do. For what I
> want to do I do not do, but what I hate I do
> (verse 15).

Every Christian can relate to this verse. We know what we are supposed to do. We really want to do it. But, like a child who can't resist touching that freshly painted bench, we simply can't help ourselves. Why?

> As it is, it is no longer I myself who do it,
> but it is sin living in me (verse 17).

When we are not filled with the Holy Spirit, we fill the void with worldly desires, or sins. We don't want to do this. We even justify it: "Just one time won't hurt. How bad can it be? It makes me feel good and that's what's important. Besides, I'm not hurting anyone else."

So we sin. Just a little one. It makes us feel good for a while, slightly filling the void inside of us. But that feeling of fulfillment is fleeting, and when it leaves, the emptiness is greater than before. The snowball has started rolling. How can we stop it? Romans, chapter 8 holds the answer:

> Those who live according to the sinful nature have their minds set on what that nature desires; but those who live in accordance with the Spirit have their minds set on what the Spirit desires. The mind of sinful man is death, but the mind controlled by the Spirit is life and peace; the sinful mind is hostile to God. It does not submit to God's law, nor can it do so. Those controlled by the sinful nature cannot please God.

Quite simply, we can't stop it. If we are controlled by our sinful nature, we cannot please God. If we cannot please God, we can't be whole. That is the way we were created. In order to be whole, we must have the Holy Spirit inside of us. There is a place for Him set aside. It cannot be adequately filled with anything from this world. That should be abundantly clear by now. However, there is very good news, as Romans, chapter 8 continues:

You, however, are controlled not by the sinful nature but by the Spirit, if the Spirit of God lives in you. And if anyone does not have the Spirit of Christ, he does not belong to Christ. But if Christ is in you, your body is dead because of sin, yet your spirit is alive because of righteousness. And if the Spirit of Him who raised Jesus from the dead is living in you, He who raised Christ from the dead will also give life to your mortal bodies through His Spirit, who lives in you.

Hope! We do not have to live a life feeling less than full and complete. If we reject the Holy Spirit, we will fail to fill that void inside of us. However, if we accept the Holy Spirit, we will be renewed and made whole.

We live in a society that encourages self-dependence and individuality. It is a sign of weakness to ask for help. The difficult thing with accepting the Holy Spirit is that we must first admit that we need Him. We need Him to become whole.

Human nature is to do what makes us feel good. We feel that if it makes us happy and it doesn't hurt anyone else, then it should be fine. That's what Adam and Eve thought, that eating the forbidden fruit would make them happy. Besides, who is it hurting, anyway?

God has a different plan for us. He is interested in our long-term joy, not our fleeting happiness. It is much like the relationship between a parent and child. My oldest son loves chicken nuggets. He is fifteen and wants to order a twenty-piece meal whenever we go to his favorite fast-food restaurant. I tell him, "You shouldn't do it. I know they taste good, but it isn't good for you."

He can't resist. I find this to be a teachable moment and indulge him. He regrets it an hour later. This is just like sin in our lives. We are warned. We do it anyway. We regret it. Then, we repeat. The next time we go to this restaurant, my son orders the twenty-piece meal (teenage boys are not the brightest of God's creations). Again, he regrets it. He can't help himself. Neither can we. We always think it will be different this time. We will have the joy but not the regret. It doesn't work that way. Not without the Holy Spirit.

Finally, the Holy Spirit exists to give us life—real, deep, meaningful life, not a life in which you are left thirsting or hungering for more. A life of fulfillment. Let's look at Biblical evidence of this fact.

John, chapter 4 tells the story of Jesus and the woman at the well. Jesus had a long day's journey and sat next to Jacob's well to rest. As He did so, a Samaritan woman came to the well to draw water. Jesus asked her for a drink. Now, since Jesus was a Jew, and because Jews and Samaritans didn't associate, the woman asked Him, "How can you ask me for water?"

Jesus responds, "If you know the gift of God and who it is that asks you for a drink, you would have

asked Him and He would have given you living water."
Understandably, the Samaritan woman is perplexed and
asks what He means by "living water." Jesus answers,
"Everyone who drinks this water will be thirsty again,
but whoever drinks the water I give him will never thirst.
Indeed, the water I give him will become in him a spring
of water welling up to eternal life."

> This thought is repeated in John, chapter 6,
> verse 35:

> I am the bread of life. He who comes to
> me will never go hungry, and he who
> believes in me will never be thirsty.

The Holy Spirit will lead us to a relationship with Jesus
Christ. When our eyes are on Him, we will never be
spiritually thirsty, hungry, or empty. We will be full. We
will be whole. How can you drink of this living water
and eat this bread? By accepting Jesus Christ into your
life through befriending His gift to us, the Holy Spirit.

Chapter 8

Spirit Love

What have we learned thus far?

- We learned why we feel empty.

- We looked at what we do to fill that emptiness.

- We learned who the Holy Spirit is.

- We learned about the purpose of the Holy Spirit.

- We learned how to invite the Holy Spirit into our lives.

- We learned what to expect when the Holy Spirit enters our lives.

- We learned why we need the Holy Spirit and the power He can have over our lives.

I would be remiss not to point out the single greatest power in the world. It has the power to turn evil men good, or good men evil. It has the power to conquer entire communities, cultures, and civilizations. It is not a weapon. It is not a person. It is not a chemical or an invention. It is love.

God is the greatest power in the universe. He created the universe and all the powers in it, for crying out loud. 1 John 4:8 states:

> Whoever does not love does not know
> God, because God is love.

Think about that. God is love. Love is something we have. We have access to the greatest power in all of creation. Love. The symbol of love in our society is marriage. The most common verse at weddings is 1 Corinthians 13:13:

> And now these three remain: faith, hope,
> and love. But the greatest of these is love.

If you have attended a wedding, you are likely familiar with the verse. Have you ever wondered why love is the greatest? Think about it. As Christians, our faith is in God through Jesus Christ. Faith is the belief in something unseen. As Christians, we believe in God. That is our *faith*. Our *hope* is in Jesus's return to take us to heaven in His second coming.

On the last day, we will be with God. He will no longer be unseen. We will no longer have need for *faith*. We will see Him! On that day, Jesus's second coming will have already occurred. We will have no more need for that *hope*. All that is left will be love. God is love.

Love was present at the beginning, and it will be all that is left at the end—God's great, unbridled love.

Love can be different things in the modern world. I love my wife. I love God. I love my children. I love my job. I love my students. I love my players. I love the Green Bay Packers. How are we to know exactly what love is? I'm not sure where I heard it, but on a podcast someone gave a description of the following four types of love that made sense to me:

1. **Baby Love**

   Give me. This is the love a pet feels for its owner and perhaps a newborn feels for his or her parents. You can provide me with something I need; therefore, I love you.

2. **Transactional Love**

   Let's make a deal. I'll love you if you love me or give me something else. You must first give me that, and then I will return that love. This is sometimes what we see in youngsters dating—I'll love you if you give me status, take me nice places, etc.

3. **Unconditional Love**

   I'll love you even if I get nothing in return. This is the type of love parents feel for their children, especially when they become teenagers and we don't feel that love coming back from them as much as we used to.

4. Spirit Love

I'll love you even if you are hurting or persecuting me.

Whoa. Easy to say, but can we honestly say that when someone is persecuting or meaning to hurt us or someone we love that we can truly love them? What does that look like? Probably the most well-known verse in the Bible is John 3:16:

> For God so loved the world that He gave His one and only Son, that whoever believes in Him shall not perish but have eternal life.

This is how much God loves us. He gave His one and only son. But there's more:

> But God demonstrates His own love for us in this: While we were still sinners, Christ died for us (Romans 5:8).

See, God doesn't just love the righteous people. God loves sinners. God loves people who slander Him and seek to keep Him out of the government and schools. God loves us. God loves you. God loves me. He loves us so much that He sent His one and only son to die for us—not when we were righteous and good, but while we were still sinners. He sent Jesus, His one and only son, to save sinners. That's Spirit love.

As human beings, it is impossible to love someone while they are vengefully trying to harm you through slander, libel, gossip, or physical or emotional abuse. Let me say that again. As humans, it is impossible for us to exhibit Spirit love. But, as Jesus said in Matthew 19:26:

> With man this is impossible, but with God
> all things are possible.

Spirit love can only be attained if the Holy Spirit resides inside of us. God wants us to have access to this Spirit love. One of Jesus's last instructions to His disciples, recorded in John 14, clarifies the magnitude of this. This is at the Last Supper with His disciples. Jesus knows He is going to die a gruesome death the next day and is therefore trying to impress upon His disciples His most important lesson:

> A new command I give you; love one
> another. As I have loved you, so you must
> love one another. By this all men will
> know that you are my disciples, if you
> love one another."

This is it. Jesus knows His time is limited. Basically, He tells His disciples this: If you forget everything else I have told you, just remember this one thing—love each other. This is how people will know you are my followers and how you will save their souls by bringing

them to me. Love them. All of them. This is Spirit love.
1 Peter, chapter 3 tells us the same lesson this way:

> Who is going to harm you if you are eager to
> do good? But even if you should suffer for
> what is right, you are blessed. "Do not fear
> what they fear; do not be frightened." But in
> your hearts set apart Christ as Lord. Always
> be prepared to give an answer to everyone
> who asks you to give the reason for the hope
> that you have. But do this with gentleness and
> respect, keeping a clear conscience, so that
> those who speak maliciously against your
> good behavior in Christ may be ashamed of
> their slander. It is better, if it is God's will,
> to suffer for doing good than for doing evil.
> For Christ died for sins once for all, the
> righteous for the unrighteous, to bring you
> to God. He was put to death in the body but
> made alive by the Spirit, through whom also
> He went and preached to the spirits in prison
> who disobeyed long ago when God waited
> patiently in the days of Noah while the ark
> was being built. In it only a few people, eight
> in all, were saved through water, and this
> water symbolizes baptism that now saves you
> also—not the removal of dirt from the body
> but the pledge of a good conscience toward
> God. It saves you by the resurrection of Jesus
> Christ, who has gone into heaven and is at

God's right hand—with angels, authorities, and powers in submission to Him.

Summed up, this is the message Peter gave in these verses to Jewish Christians who were being persecuted:

- It is better to be punished in this world for doing good than in the next for doing bad.

- Always have a spot in your heart for Jesus (the same place we have for the Holy Spirit!).

- When people ask you why you are so loving and hopeful, be prepared to witness for Jesus, but do it gently and respectfully.

- Be baptized—not to make you physically clean, but to make you spiritually clean for God.

This hope and love that others were to see in first-century Jewish Christians that were being persecuted is the same hope and love they are to see in modern-day disciples of Christ. They are to see, in all circumstances, love, joy, peace, patience, kindness, goodness, faithfulness, gentleness, and self-control. These are the fruits of the Holy Spirit as outlined in Galatians, chapter 5. The only way to exhibit these qualities in all circumstances is with the Holy Spirit residing in His designated spot in your heart.

The greatest power in all of creation is available to all of us if we will just accept it and allow it to fill its rightful place inside of us. My prayer is that everyone who reads this book will accept that power and let it transform their life. This is the only thing that can transform your life for the purpose that God has for you.

My prayer is that you will allow the Holy Spirit to make you whole.

CPSIA information can be obtained
at www.ICGtesting.com
Printed in the USA
FFOW05n2009020116